S&T Happens

Surviving and Thriving in a VUCA World

Rob England and Dr Cherry Vu

Sensible business practices

Created by Two Hills Ltd (trading as Teal Unicorn™)

letterbox@twohills.co.nz
www.twohiolls.co.nz
PO Box 57-150, Mana
Porirua 5247
New Zealand

© Copyright Two Hills Ltd 2022

Published by Two Hills Ltd
Version 1.6, April 2022
Unless otherwise credited, all photos and diagrams are by the authors.
The moral rights of the authors are asserted.
All Rights Reserved. No part of this publication may be reproduced, stored in a retrieval system, or transmitted, in any form or by any means, electronic, mechanical, photocopying, recording or otherwise, without prior permission of the authors.
Although this book has been carefully prepared, neither the authors nor the publisher accepts any liability for damages caused by any error or omission of this book. We make no claim that the use of any aspect of this book will assure a successful outcome.
Use of any trademarks in this document is not intended in any way to infringe on the rights of the trademark holder.
The Two Hills logo, "Teal Unicorn", and The Teal Unicorn logo are trademarks of Two Hills Ltd.

In our last book, *Open Management*, the first-person pronoun "I" was used to refer to Teal Unicorn, to both Cherry and Rob. This was done to avoid confusion since "we" is also used as a collective reference to all readers of the book. I/we didn't like that approach, so in this book I/we use "TU" as an abbreviation of Teal Unicorn, and try to avoid referring to ourselves by pronouns entirely.

Dedicated to those dealing with a chaotic world right now.

May you know better times.

Contents

S&T Happens 1
- Personal journeys 1
- What TU found 4
- Meet Mr Teal 6
- It's a VUCA world 8

S&T through adaptability 15
- Agility 18
- Resilience 19
- Efficiency and Optimisation 23

S&T with better ways of managing 25

S&T with Open Planning 31
- Planning is waste 35
- So if we don't plan, what do we do? 38
- Plan n cycles in the short term. 39
- Vision n years out. 42
- Scenario analysis 48
- Goals 58
- Projects 58
- Direction 60
- Roadmap 60
- Control 61

Better ways to advance our capability 63
- Growing capability 63
- Advancing the system of work 66
- Thriving on adversity and opportunity 74

Afterword 79

S&T Happens

2020 changed everything. It is an inflection point in history. There is no going back. Nor is there a new normal state to settle into. Change, accelerating change, is the new normal state.

How can we survive and thrive[1] ("S&T Happens" - what did you think it meant?) in a world marked by volatility, uncertainty, complicatedness, and ambiguity? ("VUCA", more of that later).

Surviving and thriving in such a world requires an organisation to be constantly adaptable - meaning resilient and agile. We must cope and change.

We survive by mitigating risk and absorbing shocks (resilience), and we thrive by capitalising quickly on new opportunities (agility). As you will see, we change how we see the future, and how we plan for it.

Personal journeys

Please indulge personal reflections from Rob and Cherry here. Both are relevant. First from Cherry:

As I look back on these pandemic years, I want to remember the silent battle as we strive to live and work in a 'new normal'. Here's what I've learned over the past two years:

In March 2020, I took my last flight back to NZ after a business trip in Vietnam. The world has been closed since then. I spent three days being sad, thinking about what I should do and feeling bewildered. But soon I learned resilience by diving into learning the skills, tools, and methods so I could continue to do the things that matter to me. Our entire operating model has changed, and we've done more than ever

---

[1] This may be where we got the Surviving and Thriving phrase from originally https://centricconsulting.com/blog/surviving-and-thriving-in-a-vuca-world_st_louis/

in the past two years. Organising big international events online, or training thousands of leaders and managers, as well as consulting completely remotely was previously unthinkable. Thanks to Covid, we have completed six books in two years.

The past two years have taught me that it is not enough for me to want to make a change, to bring good things to the people around me and to society, and consider them as the right values. As I develop a business agility community and a parent community, I understand more than ever that building a community requires more than love and care, I need to devote my time and energy to it.

When the crisis hit, I learned that acceptance is liberating. Completely abandoning the illusion of control or domination over anything, we need to discover what's going on and go with the flow, instead of resisting it or trying to think we can control it. We are not certain of anything about the future, nor can we control everything. The only thing we can do is do the best we can in the present moment, and be prepared for whatever happens in the future.

I have learned that I prefer solitude to being busy commuting from one flight to another, from one country to another. I still enjoy interacting with people but have found a lot of beauty in the stillness. When my mind was quiet, I was able to write more, work more efficiently, and live slower.

I learned that no judgement is valid for survival, and that people are always just doing what they can achieve the way they know how. I'm happy to help someone realising they don't know what they don't know, and I'm always open to expanding my understanding.

Over the past two years, many aspects of our lives have stalled and even frozen, but I believe we've all learned one thing: we need to care about what's really important to us.

And a reflection from Rob:

In 2005, my fit active 70-year-old father sat down in a chair and died. My 30-year-old neighbour sat in his van to go to work and did the same thing.

After 16 years at the same corporate employer, I quit my job to make a living independently on this new thing, the internet.

I quickly realised that the big money was still in real world consulting, so I spent the next 12 years at that, while still hunting for that elusive online income. I grew in my capabilities and shifted areas from time to time, but it was a steady trajectory.

In 2013 my marriage failed, and I was a solo parent. I spiralled into dangerous depression, but nothing at work changed until I came to a breaking point in 2016. I went onto medication, and suddenly life changed direction. All in one year, my son got his life going, my long-lost daughter turned up, I met Cherry, and we started a new business, Teal Unicorn ("TU"). For 2 years Cherry and I forged a new direction, consulting and teaching business agility in Vietnam. Life was wonderful, literally the best years of my life. I was mapping the next 5 to 10 years: both of us consulting in two countries, steadily increasing the Vietnam business until TU moved there for a couple of years, building Cherry's side of the business before I get too old (she's a bit younger), then retire to NZ…

At the end of 2019, I got cancer and couldn't do much work (luckily there wasn't much business agility work around in NZ). Then COVID hit and Cherry and I couldn't go to Vietnam anymore. TU pivoted to online training from home, which is rapidly growing for us in a crowded market, thanks to DrVu's brilliance.

After a year of that, it occurred to us that TU could do this from anywhere with a decent internet. So TU bought a caravan.

As awareness of the effectiveness of Cherry's ideas grew in Vietnam, she rapidly expanded into C-level corporate coaching and consulting, changing our business patterns yet again.

See a trend? Pivoting after 16 years... 12... 4... 2... 2021 was wildly different to 2020 for us, and now 2022 shifts again with war in Europe (and on the internet), and the reopening of Vietnam to travel. TU are adapting constantly

What TU found

Teal Unicorn has done a lot of thinking and learning about how to cope with a crazy world. Many say this is the new normal: no normal. It's not going to go back to the way it was. The post-WW2 years in Western countries - and the global economy - were, historically, exceptionally stable and peaceful. We have been in an "interbellum" period. That's unlikely to resume post-pandemic as the Ukraine invasion - at the time of writing - makes clear. VUCA is here to stay. You may be doing great or you may be struggling, but one thing is clear: **what got you here won't get you there**. How do we flex and writhe to survive and thrive? TU have been learning, and it is turning out rather well for us and for our clients (fingers crossed). To survive and thrive:

1. We need more adaptable ways of working. These ways arise from new ways of thinking about work.

2. Better ways of working require better ways of managing.

3. Planning looks very different once we admit we are not psychic.

4. We use these better ways to advance our capability safely.

5. We learn to capitalise on turbulence and failure.

With these practices, you don't just survive, you can thrive. One can surf the disruptive forces to find new opportunities that open up. Turbulence – even chaos – doesn't have to be a bad thing if you are prepared for it, if your confidence is high, your systems are resilient, and your work is agile.

At the same time as we deal with VUCA, social change is afoot. There is a global enlightenment happening, exploring better ways of thinking[2].

So as well as building resilience and agility, we can take a higher ground in social evolution. Find better solutions for the outcomes for the workers and for the community, not just the organisation and its owners. You can be among the first going there, to be better and do better than other organisations. It's not that you out-compete as a result - one wants to rise above such thinking. As a social leader, you pull others up with you, and you become the natural hub of the network.

To bring the two parts of this section together: greater enlightenment within the organisation helps resilience and agility dealing with a VUCA world. Staff are empowered[3], creative, and confident.

It works for Teal Unicorn. More importantly, it works for our clients. TU are not just surviving a pandemic, we are thriving.

---

[2] https://tealunicorn.com/nwot
[3] You know what: let's stop saying "empowered". I've been uncomfortable with "empower" for some time, but I keep habitually using it. Daniel Mezick taught us that distributing authority is not about giving power in a patronising hierarchical fashion, empowering. Then the authority contains the potential to take it back at will. If you liberate people, there is no taking it back.
A while back, I came up with a word I prefer: "liberating".

Meet Mr Teal

Meet Mr Teal. He's a caravan.

In this context, "Teal" is a level of social advancement, the highest so far achieved[4]. It is part of the language of new ways of working. It's part of our brand, Teal Unicorn.

The Unicorn part is about the ultimate operating model. A "Unicorn" is a real organisation that does things indistinguishable from magic.

This book asserts that much conventional planning is waste. TU calls the alternative Open Planning. Part of that alternative is scenarios. TU tests the model on ourselves: the caravan is an option for several scenarios in our future.

Strategy is generally more stable than its operational implementation: one needs adaptability more at the day-to-day level. But strategy must also be able to change direction quickly in response to changing external conditions. It may not happen as often as the need to adjust at the local level of work, but it will happen, and it will be essential for organisational survival, and the ability to opportunistically take advantage of the shift.

The increasingly unpredictable future is going to need greater adaptability[5].

Adaptability = Agility + Resilience

Sticking doggedly to a long-term strategy in the face of a changing reality is a losing game, as much as adhering to an obsolete operational plan. An operating model might need to adapt often, even as a strategy remains the same. Then, when strategy needs to change quickly, an adaptable operating model enables it.

Mr Teal the caravan is about agility. He gives TU a number of options to employ in response to a range of possible scenarios. He allows us to respond quickly, at short notice.

---

[4] The term "teal" comes to us from the book *Reinventing Organizations* by Frederic Laloux.
[5] We forget the origin of this "equation". The combination crops up quite often.

Mr Teal is also about resilience. A few of you will know what the figurehead is. It's a kevlar-mesh radiotherapy mask. They bolted me (Rob) down to a table with it 35 times to get rid of my tongue and lymph cancers. So far so good: I'm fit again.

So Mr Teal stands as a symbol at the intersection of TU personal and business lives. He's about agility and resilience in future. Onward.

Watch "Meet Mr Teal" on YouTube: https://youtu.be/59m59jhJNYI

It's a VUCA world

The world is increasingly VUCA: "Volatile, Uncertain, Complex, and Ambiguous".

Not everyone has heard the term VUCA but its use is increasing. Over 30 years old, it has been used by the military to describe the new geopolitical world, and increasingly it is used day to day to describe our lived experience. If you aren't aware of VUCA yet, google it. This book is not about giving you yet another potted history.

Teal Unicorn slightly changed the wording of VUCA to volatile, uncertain, compli**cated**, and ambiguous. When the military coined the term VUCA, they used "complex" to mean having too many moving parts to be able to figure it out. The nearest it comes to what one these days thinks of as "complex" is in recognising the lack of understanding of cause-and-effect. Don't confuse complexity (as in the sense of complex adaptive systems) with complicatedness. That's why TU changed it. Developing a vaccine is complicated. What the virus does is complex. As a result, the virus's progress is VUCA.

>It is volatile: the data changes unpredictably.

>It is uncertain: will we find a safe vaccine and when? Will it mutate?

>It is complicated: there is a global network of infection, lockdowns, treatment, travel…

It is ambiguous: What is the IFR? How does it transmit? Do masks work?

Complexity gives rise to VUCA conditions. VUCA adds up to complex.

Complexity arises from a network of relationships between autonomous agents (that is TU's best understanding so far). It is not the sum of its parts, it is the product of their interactions. That quickly becomes impossible to analyse. VUCA are emergent descriptive properties of the resulting system.

> Complexity is not a higher form of complicatedness
>
> – Sonja Blignaut

In complex systems, it is impossible to know the whole current system, the whole change that will happen, or the future state at any point in time, because it is VUCA.

For the last century of management (of government and industry), they used an approximation of the world that said it was simple and linear: a known input gives a known result - we can discover and model cause-and-effect. Even as they understood more about the complex nature of the world, the approximation worked, so long as change was slow enough that the lag between input and output didn't cause huge errors, and so long as information was good enough that one could see something of what lies ahead. The assumption here is that reality won't have changed much from when we define what we are going to do until when we finish doing it. In most domains, that is no longer true except for over short timeframes. The idea of simple predictable linear systems is no longer close enough. "Define Once, Execute Perfectly" is a fallacy. The future is unknown. The only way to know is to do. Conventional project management with its time-frames measured in quarters and years has been called "delivering last year's requirements". It may have worked in the past but less so now. What got you here won't get you there.

Treating the world as predictable was always an approximation. It worked when the pace of change was low. The target didn't move in the time it took to get there. Now our targets leap around like mad things. We often talk about navigational stars to guide us, but this is a misleading analogy. When sailing, we pick a star because all stars move slowly and predictably. Our "stars" in the modern world are more like fireflies. You look away for a moment and your target isn't there anymore.

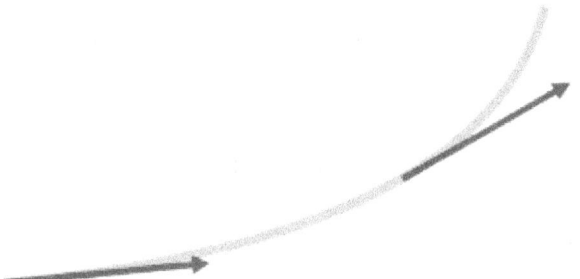

Of course, the world never was stable. Life blindsides you. But conventionally, we would treat that as unforeseeable, the unexpected, surprising, an act of god. We would treat it as exceptional. It's not. It is normal for random things to happen – the world is random. The myth of predictability was only ever a mental model. Now it is becoming impossible to ignore the reality. We must adjust to expecting the unexpected, the "black swan"[6]. We must act on the assumption that we don't know what the world is going to be. The future is disordered, foggy, unpredictable.

Image origin unknown

---

[6] Introduced in a book by Nicolas Taleb of the same name.

There are multiple reasons why the world is increasingly VUCA, but the primary one, probably driving all the others, is the accelerating rate of progress in technology[7], especially in three domains: digital, biological, and materials. The biggest impact of this is sociological; society can't adapt to the new physical environment as fast as that environment changes. So new technologies are disrupting all our social structures and behaviours, from government and politics to education and reading. For example, we can't agree on the codes of behaviour in the new context of the internet. Regulation emerges only in response to problems once they become unbearable. And so on – you know the story. How does work deal with a VUCA world?

One movement that is stumbling along behind this technological curve is an advance in thinking about how we manage that technology. It's the topic of another book someday. We have moved through stages (you can see this in multiple domains such as agriculture, railways, medicine, or IT). We advance through ever-wider areas:

- Things: stuff, objects, the components.
- Practices to work the things: processes, rules, behaviours.
- People who execute the practices: culture, teams, leadership.
- Systems made up of the interactions of people, practices and things: networks, emergence, complexity.
- Values applied to and expected of those systems: ethics, humanity, inclusion.

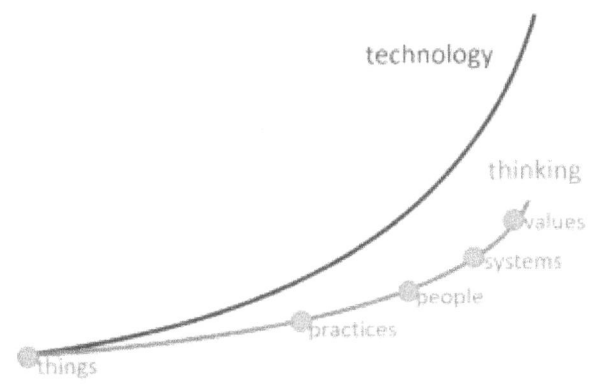

---

[7] E.g. https://www.visualcapitalist.com/the-history-of-innovation-cycles/

Here we find a crossover into the other major driver of change, the social enlightenment discussed in TU's book *Open Management*. As one's scope expands to include values, we think about the social context and impact of our systems. Lately, society has evolved to expect and demand ESG policy (environmental, social, and governance issues). Now the pandemic is shining a light on how staff are treated.

Along with accelerating technology and social enlightenment, a third reason the world seems increasingly VUCA is our growing understanding of the world as systems. Near the end of the last millennium, we finally developed some rigour in understanding that those systems are *complex*, in a strict mathematical sense of the word. This leads to awareness of some basic principles of complexity:

- We can never know the whole of a system.
- We can never model or predict what it will do.
    - There is no function relating the inputs to the outputs.
    - The same input can result in a different output on a different occasion.
    - Success and failure can happen the same way.
- We cannot predict what will happen when we make a change.
    - Zero risk is impossible
    - S&&t happens (two ampersands). Failure is normal.
- There are emergent behaviours we cannot predict. Some of them we cannot explain.
- The system responds to its environment - it is never a closed system[8]. A complex system may not be alive, but it often acts as if it is.

---

[8] Boundaries of a real-world system are only a mental construct, they have no reality. Where does a mountain start?

- Everybody sees the system differently; we all have a different model in our head.

The stereotypical example of a complex system is the weather. With massive amounts of study, huge lakes of data, and awesome computer processing power, we can have a pretty good idea of the weather for a week. It still occasionally surprises us. Beyond that, we talk in trends and probabilities, and in a great aggregate: the climate. Again, we have a pretty good idea of the climate next year, but the wide ranges in the IPCC projections[9] show that extrapolation of a complex system is a fool's game. It is hubris to think we understand the causality. We fit models to the past data, but they hold little knowledge of the future. Nobody really knows what the effect of melting ice caps or changing albedo will be. They're in the model as educated guesses, not validated by any data. You don't know until you do: until you do get there, or until you do something and see the effect.

If we truly understand these principles, then they radically change how we think. If we tightly bound the system and keep it simple, (usually with computer programs, or with concrete and machines), then a simple linear model can be used, such as a factory production schedule, a process flow, or a value stream map. But again, it is only a model and it was always an approximation of reality – the myth of the simple system. Not only is the future murky, but so is the present. It is not under the control we think it is. We could lose that simplicity anytime. The bounds we set have their limits. A simple linear bounded system is always fragile. For my favourite example, search YouTube for steel mill accidents. Molten or red-hot metal is kept tightly within machine bounds… until it's not.

It's a complex VUCA world. We must learn to deal with it. That's what the better ways of thinking, working, and managing are about.

---

[9] https://www.ipcc.ch/report/ar4/wg1/global-climate-projections/

S&T through adaptability

2020 changed the game for organisations, whether business, not-for-profit, or government. We need different ways of working. What got you here won't get you there. To survive and thrive (S&T) going forward, we need adaptability.

Work has changed forever. Teal Unicorn embrace remote working. TU can do all our work in our caravan, from Zoom meetings to printing and scanning contracts. For the ultimate in remote working, watch "Dr Vu Goes to Work" on YouTube: https://youtu.be/nqkPE0HQ3GI

Once Mr Musk gets his satellites dense enough to serve mountain valleys, this hut shown here will be our third office (along with home and the caravan):

Of course, it's not just about remote working, that is only a tiny part of the shift. To cope with a volatile, uncertain, complicated, and ambiguous world, one needs more adaptable ways of working. Remote working is one symptom of much bigger changes beneath. Ways of working that got you to this point may have worked fine, but most organisations are struggling to make their existing operating models work in this decade, and many more will meet challenges soon.

Image © Copyright CanStockPhoto.com

Treating the world as made up of defined repeatable work (Taylorism, CMMI, Lean Six Sigma, ITIL...) or made up of flowing left-to-right streams (Lean, ToC, project management, IT's DevOps...) are simplified approximations of reality that only have acceptable levels of error when the world is sufficiently stable over time. That is becoming rarer.

Lean and Theory of Constraints (ToC) are effective in a factory production line, and IT Continuous Delivery works for enterprise software deployment, because these are highly bounded systems where linear flow approximations still work. Beware of using them in other contexts, and always be aware of the vulnerability of the simple system.

You can't statistically measure work (or variation in work) when every transaction is different - you need it defined, standardised, and repeatable to measure (or automate). You can't quantify much about knowledge work because it is invisible - the value produced is intangible and often unquantifiable. You can't measure individuals when output is created by collaborating groups - the contribution of one person is often not understood until they're gone, as many ill-considered layoffs have shown. You can't optimise flow unless it is in a steady(-ish) state, or at least predictable, mathematically modelled. You can't model flow when it exists in a complicated network of autonomous co-creating agents. You can't apply models and measures to a system where cause and effect are unknown. (Lack of causality is a defining attribute of a complex system. Reality is a complex system.)

These complex systems are VUCA. You can't know what they are doing with precision, nor predict what they will do next with any certainty.

To handle this reality, let's return to the "equation" Adaptability = Agility + Resilience.

Agility

Business Agility is well documented. Teal Unicorn calls all the ways of working - that broadly get lumped together as "agility" - as "better ways of managing and working". TU are trying to move away from that word "new", both because it has baggage, and because many of them aren't. Or TU say "Open Management and Open Work" because TU see "open" as a better word than "agile" in future.

TU summarise all the concepts associated with Open Work as Human Systems Adaptability:

- bringing humanity to work[10],
- creating flow and flexibility[11],
- and exploring our work safely[12].

(The links are to our articles on these topics).

One part of Open Work is indeed agility. TU summarise the behaviours of agility as:

- **Iterate**: work in short, repeated cycles
- **Increment**: produce small units of work, proceed in small steps
- **Experiment**: every increment is an experiment - you don't know for sure until you try. So minimise risk.
- **Explore**: accept that the result is unknowable. Find your way.

The more local the focus, the more agile one must be, because change is faster and variability greater on smaller scales. Agility is an operational capability enabled in teams. The more that we can have many small teams with minimum coupling between them, the more agile we can be. For an organisation to be highly agile, we must maximise the decomposition into smaller units of work.

---

[10] https://tealunicorn.com/rediscovering-and-restoring-humanity/
[11] https://tealunicorn.com/st-fluidity
[12] https://tealunicorn.com/nwomaw

Agility is also required at the large scale, the macro view, in strategy and organisational planning. It's a more sedate process but the same concepts apply: iterate, increment, experiment, explore. Be prepared to fail, be prepared to adapt.

Resilience

Business Resilience is less trendy than Business Agility - less is said about it right now.

Resilience can mean[13]:

1. **rebound**: "rebounds from disrupting or traumatic events and returns to previous or normal activities"
2. **robustness**: "is able to manage increasing complexity, stressors, and challenge"
3. graceful **extensibility**: "extends performance, or brings extra adaptive capacity to bear, when surprise events challenge its boundaries"
4. Many people also include **adaptability** as an aspect of resilience. In this book TU have it the other way around, with resilience as one aspect of adaptability.

Resilience is the ability to come back from setbacks and grow from the experience, in other words: organisational antifragility[14].

Resilience Engineering is building work systems to be resilient: ensuring that our people and systems cope, recover, and grow stronger when things go wrong.

Business Resilience refers to:

---

[13] *Four concepts for resilience and the implications for the future of resilience engineering*, D.D. Woods, Safety Science.
[14] Nicolas Taleb created the concept of antifragile in a book of the same name. I find the book unreadable but the concept is brilliant. Read more here https://teaunicorn.com/antifragile/

- the resilience of business systems to survive stress, to heal, to recover, and to grow stronger as a result (antifragile) by learning with intention. Get organised: be ready for anything that happens now, be prepared. Assume it will go wrong. Expect human error. Expect Black Swans[15]. Expect catastrophe. Make systems fail safe, self healing, evolutionary, anything to better survive failures. Stop:
    - building fragile systems that only work when everything goes right.
    - ...especially "Tarzan" systems that let you swing out into space on the assumption that the next vine is there to grab.
    - optimising out all the buffers of material in the name of Just In Time efficiency.
    - optimising all the capacity out in the name of utilisation.
    - dragging legacy systems debt along in the name of ROI or sunk cost.
    - expecting humans to get it right every time.
- the resilience of our people to cope with adversity, to have: reserves of capacity and energy to deal with the unplanned; positive attitudes and morale; optimism; confidence; a sense of strength and capability.
- the resilience of our culture which embraces adversity as growth, challenge as opportunity, failure as normal learning, and destruction as a refresh.

Volatility, uncertainty, complicatedness, and ambiguity are the new normal. In a VUCA world, how can we be more resilient to their impact?[16] That way, VUCA can be a positive stimulus to the organisation, not a negative force.

Here are some tactics[17]:

---

[15] Another great concept from Taleb, also in a book of the same name, also unreadable.
[16] https://sloanreview.mit.edu/article/how-autonomy-creates-resilience-in-the-face-of-crisis/
[17] The first four points (manage, navigate, reduce, clarify) are derived from Bennett, Nathan; Lemoine, G. James. *"What VUCA Really Means to You."*

- Manage volatility. Build in slack and devote resources to preparedness. Put another way, don't strip out your systems too much (don't cut to the bone), and make sure you value response capabilities that are sometimes idle.

- Navigate uncertainty. Invest in information; collect, interpret and share it. Encourage diversity, liberation[18], and collaboration in understanding information.

- Reduce complicatedness. Simplify. Abstract and virtualise. Decouple: remove dependencies, create autonomy, break systems down into simpler smaller parts. Pay down systems debt.

- Clarify ambiguity. Experiment, explore, and learn. Build sense-making[19] capability to understand situations. Grow collaboration to widen the context as much as possible.

- Build business intelligence capability (sensors to detect data changes, streams of curated information from outside, networks of contacts to detect disturbances, tracking trends and incoming possibilities) to foresee or quickly detect as much as possible. I.e. develop "radar".

- Create an organisation founded on commitment to continuous learning and improvement. This must be at the heart of all work. In other words: agility.

- Shape your ways of working around experimentation, and iteration in increments - many small steps. Another way of saying this is continual improvement, i.e. agility again.

- Understand the space that you are exploring. Determine your current state; understand the boundaries of the possible; what

---

Harvard Business Review. January-February 2014.
[18] See what TU did there. We didn't say "empowerment".
[19] "Sense-making" is a wonderful word for the techniques for trying to know as much as we can about our uncertain ambiguous situation. More about it later in this book.

the constraints are and what additional constraints you can create. The classic example of a bounding constraint is a legal limit. The classic example of an enabling constraint that one imposes on ourselves to make work better is to limit the amount of work in progress.

- Build critical-thinking skills. Be able to detect and compensate for biases, to challenge and dismantle assumptions and principles, and to debate respectfully and productively.

- Grow a culture of positivity and confidence. Resilience breeds resilience. Every time we bounce back, we build our preparedness for next time.

- Build systems that cope, recover, and improve. This is what many people think of as Resilience Engineering, but as you can see above, it is only one part of the story. Disciplines such as Disaster Recovery, Business Continuity, Major Incident Response, and Systems Reliability cover this aspect well.

If we aren't resilient, it should be clear that we will build systems debt[20] when things don't get fixed properly, when we incur damage, when we don't recover well. And we will build cultural debt if morale takes a hammering, and people get stressed, pessimistic, exhausted, and burnt out.

If we agree to move toward more adaptability, we must make the journey in an adaptable way too, using these new ways to experiment and explore forward, advancing safely.

Teal Unicorn likes to promote experiment programmes to encourage teams to try new behaviours. They grow confidence that a behaviour or activity or tool works, that they are capable, and that it will be rewarded. As a group, we find out what works, we spread capability, and we improve.

---

[20] IT calls it technical debt.

Efficiency and Optimisation

Conventional managers will be noting the lack of discussion of efficiency and optimisation, wondering where they fit.

Increasing efficiency is good when it makes us lighter - when we shed bureaucracy, reduce waste, increase velocity - so that we can be more responsive to change.

An excessive focus on efficiency, however, leads to over-optimised systems that are fragile under changing circumstances if there is no slack in the system to deal with disruption. As I write this, the world's supply chains are still wrecked two years into the COVID pandemic. There was too much Just In Time supply, with insufficient buffers, and too many exclusive suppliers, with insufficient redundancy.

Continual improvement is not the same thing as optimising efficiency. It is about maintaining (and improving) effectiveness under changing circumstances. The goals keep moving and we keep adapting.

> *The 21st Century is a different game with different rules... The pursuit of efficiency was once a laudable goal, but being effective in today's world is less a question of optimizing for a known (and relatively stable) set of variables than responsiveness to a constantly shifting environment. Adaptability, not efficiency, must become our central competence.*
>
> *- Gen. Stanley McChrystal*

There is nothing wrong with making work leaner and improving flow. It's just not the end game anymore, and we must be careful not to overdo it. Adaptability can sometimes be less efficient in order to remain more effective.

Resilience requires waste. People get upset about waste of perishable food, but wasted food is essential to create dependable supply lines and to ensure freshness. It is the necessary slack in the system.

Resilience requires redundancy. Here is a story from my past. Money is always short in public health, so they didn't want to pay for duplicate data storage in a new digital radiology imaging system. Redundancy would double the cost, so they saved to tape instead. When the inevitable finally happened and the digital version was lost, it took six weeks to completely restore from tape. Digital X-rays are huge files. Redundancy is expensive but not as expensive as a lost system.

Agility requires decoupling. Some organisations store your address in multiple places, with the risk of inconsistent data, which can be infuriating. But having all your systems share one identity database creates dependencies that can create a drag on agility. It is expensive to run behind-the-scenes consistency processes to clean up multiple versions of the data, but worth it to free up change.

Agility encourages iteration over the same work, known as rework or refactoring. Build it once then build it better. This seems wasteful to conventional thinking. Why not do it all once and do it right? Because the goals keep shifting. And because we learn as we build. It's not wasteful to experiment and fail, as long as you learn.

Note that there is also a distinction between efficiency and cost cutting. A pursuit of lower costs, especially lower headcount, is almost always harmful to resilience and agility (and performance). Lower cost can be a beneficial side effect of efficiency or agility, sometimes, but it should never be the goal. And don't count on it. When you work better, you often need to work more, doing the thing you have been neglecting (usually left undone because of past cost-cutting).

S&T with better ways of managing

The understanding that agility is essential in a VUCA world is now widespread. What isn't widespread yet is the realisation that, to get to agile work, you need better ways of managing[21]. TU wrote about it in our two other books *The agile Manager (small a)*, and *Open Management*, available on Amazon

In summary, you have to let the people do the work, and create the conditions so that they want to. Only liberated workers can be agile. We can only invite them, not force them. Managers are the lock and key to new ways of working.

Managing change is not just about getting acceptance of the change. We have to let go of command-and-control. Let the people doing the

---

[21] https://tealunicorn.com/nwom

work design the work. Management should observe, navigate, and facilitate. People should be the change, not just concede to it.

Conventionally, we believed managers (or consultants) should be able to "make" things happen to plan. So managers tried, then made a big noise when they fluked it, and faked it when they didn't (because failure was unacceptable). Thinking in simpler, deterministic terms has always been an approximation, but one we got away with in a simpler, more stable world. Less so these days. In a given situation, the only way to know what is correct is to experiment, therefore we cannot assert superior knowledge except with hindsight. All human systems are "suck it and see": nobody knows.

Also conventionally, employees accepted that theatre was normal, pretending an unreal result for appearances' sake. Coercion by bosses was also normal: anger, bullying, punishment, overwork. Unethical pursuit of that which you don't personally believe in was normal: want a job, suck it up. We don't buy that anymore.

Management got away with coercion more often in the past because the more stable world allowed them to hold constraints in place to make people do what was needed. E.g. project management and its emphasis on measurement over time. A VUCA world changes too fast[22], so those constraints fail. In a stable world, the approximation that says work is simple, linear, constrained, and predictable, was near enough. The error between theatre and reality was small over time. As the world goes faster, forced knowledge work is too slow and constrained.

You can still force "transactional" workers to work[23]: farming, labourers, pieceworkers, factory, clerical… anyone who repeats a defined task over and over. If you can measure them then you can force them, and still get productivity. It doesn't work for knowledge workers. If they're unhappy, you get slow, low-quality work. As the proportion of knowledge work is rising in the service economy, and

---

[22] https://tealunicorn.com/its-a-vuca-world/
[23] http://bostonreview.net/race/caitlin-c-rosenthal-how-slavery-inspired-modern-business-management

now the information economy, bosses are (finally) waking up to the need to do what employees want and believe in, and to let it be fun. You don't make people work, you invite them. You have more success that way.

The movement to new ways of work[24] is real - it is visible everywhere. Knowledge workers are being liberated to do great work. It gives TU hope of success, better lives, and social change. TU see it in our clients[25].

You have to let the people do the work, and want to do it. Only liberated knowledge workers can be agile. Less widely accepted is that this need for liberation includes transactional workers too. It might look like they repeat the same task, which allows coercion, but not anymore. Transactional work changes. They need to be agile too. Customers expect flexibility. There are many options. Our complicated systems are always throwing exceptions. Which leads to the discovery that transactional workers are a lot smarter than their bosses give them credit for. Once they're liberated, they can contribute far more than sweat. E.g. read about Nucor Steel in Hamel and Zanini's *Humanocracy*.

When all workers are liberated to do the work they want to do, believe in, share a vision for, then we get maximum agility (and resilience), which gives organisations the adaptability to survive and thrive in a VUCA world.

The end game is amazing: ultimately those who own the organisation set it free to allow those working in it to make it their organisation, to collectively decide its Why, and unite to go there. TU are not sure of any organisation that truly does that yet (Buurtzorg come close[26]) but the trajectory of Teal[27] is clear. You can see it coming soon.

---

[24] https://tealunicorn.com/nwomaw
[25] Case studies are here https://tealunicorn.com/clients
[26] https://www.theguardian.com/social-care-network/2017/may/09/buurtzorg-dutch-model-neighbourhood-care
[27] https://en.wikipedia.org/wiki/Teal_organisation

To summarise so far:

- The world is more volatile, uncertain, complicated, and ambiguous than before. Simplifications of reality, such as linear flow models, don't work as much.
- The future is unknowable, and the behaviour of a complex system is unpredictable.
- The consequences of any action can only be discovered by doing it.
- Society is moving into a more humanistic view of work, which makes many organisational and management behaviours unacceptable.
- To survive and thrive, organisations must be more adaptable, which is a combination of agility and resilience.
- Better ways of working aren't possible until management unlock them, through better ways of managing.
- TU wrote about these better ways of working and of managing in our other books.

The rest of this book focuses on the planning aspect, and specifically the impact of these ideas on conventional planning. We look at the alternatives, and how to get to them.

S&T with Open Planning

In complex systems, it is impossible to know the whole current system, the whole change that will happen, or the future state at any point in time, because the world is VUCA. Yet we can survive and thrive: S&T happens.

> There is a one-hour video discussing many of the ideas here and their context: https://youtu.be/8lGhvPMc6o8

To survive and thrive, one adopts new patterns of ~~planning~~ preparing for the future, based on the pattern of the (Toyota) Improvement Kata:

1. Vision further forward in time than you normally do, and more about *who* we want to be that *what*, and more about generalities than specifics about what and where. Maintain a regularly refreshed strategy to get there. Understand that any thinking about this far future is a bet, nothing more.

2. Accept the VUCA nature of the current state.

    a. Adopt sense-making tools to get the best understanding of it.

    b. Make decisions at the last responsible moment. The smaller the decision, the sooner it should be happening.

    c. Likewise doing work: do small work for near term needs.

    d. Determine what outcomes to do right now in response to needs, problems, or threats, with a general direction set by our vision.

3. Use scenario analysis to develop a portfolio of options we can draw on if need be in the future. Determine what outcomes we can do right now to prepare those options.

4. Set targets only as far ahead as we have good visibility, the foreseeable future. (The rigidity of building big changes forces us to plan further out. We must accept the uncertainty of that.). Seek outcomes not outputs, what not how. Determine what outcomes they specify.

5. We now have three sets of outcomes we want, for Now, Options, and Targets. Prioritise them in a backlog. Don't have fixed plans to get to the outcomes. Probe and sense by doing experiments.

In this book, TU call this Open Planning, to tie in with our book *Open Management*.

There is a saying that we cross the river by feeling the stones under our feet. We can see the other side of the river but we must explore our way by testing each step, by experiment. When the river is calm and low, we can often see where our next steps are going as we move forward, for a certain distance ahead, but we still cannot see every step of the way to the other side of the river. When the river is moving fast and high, it is opaque with mud and we can see little or nothing, only probe and feel. And there is heightened danger of being knocked over and swept away. We must test each stone before we put our weight on it to make sure it won't roll. If you are trained for this, you know you should never do this alone, but always in a team arm-in-arm, so that when one person inevitably stumbles, we are linked and the others hold them up.

The idea of simple predictable linear systems no longer works. "Define Once, Execute Perfectly" is a fallacy. The future is unknown. The only way to know is to do, to start feeling your way across the river.

I banned my kids from saying the phrase: "I thought you said…." Yes. Yes I did say that. That was then. Things change.

At one of TU's very large clients, their training department did annual planning, but the actuality never looked even close to the plan. It was really just a ritual to get funding each year. Every year they spent several months on the plan with a huge expense to develop it. TU persuaded them to stop doing that. Now, every two months they make a schedule of training for people who want it and are available. After two months, the deviation from the plan is very small.

Another client also spent a huge amount on annual budgeting, but still required approval of every expenditure, because of their accounting rules. Besides, the expenditure in reality was always very different from the original plan, so the planning made no sense, it was a redundant effort. With our guidance, they decided not to do budgeting at all. They get together iteratively as an organisation to see what they're going to do next, how much money they should spend. They took all unnecessary planning ceremony out of the system. There is no budget or allocated funds, just policy to guide spending, and one manager approving it.

There are popular sayings that are variations of "planning is essential but plans are expendable". The thought exercise of planning is valuable to sort our ideas, but the resulting plan won't exist unchanged for long. Even in a regular task, the world no longer sits still. The essential element in plan predictability is now how long a task takes, not how familiar it is.

Note: TU uses a narrow definition of planning to mean defining a specific outcome and a sequence of steps to achieve it, often with a timeframe and milestones. A plan is "this is what we are gonna do". TU don't mean a strategy, i.e. an approach to the future, which is often called a plan[28], nor any other open-ended uses of the word. That vision of who we want to be, and what big bets we are willing to take on in the future, and a strategy to get there, are essential. But this book doesn't call it planning.

So if we don't plan beyond a near horizon of predictability, the **Foreseeable**, what do we do? We do Open Planning. We start with our vision of a **Far Future.** Then we diverge into all the possibilities in the **Zone of Uncertainty**. Then we converge onto what to do now in

---

[28]   https://hbr.org/amp/2018/08/6-steps-to-make-your-strategic-plan-really-strategic

the Foreseeable, for immediate needs, foreseeable targets, and scenario options preparations. Then plan to do that.

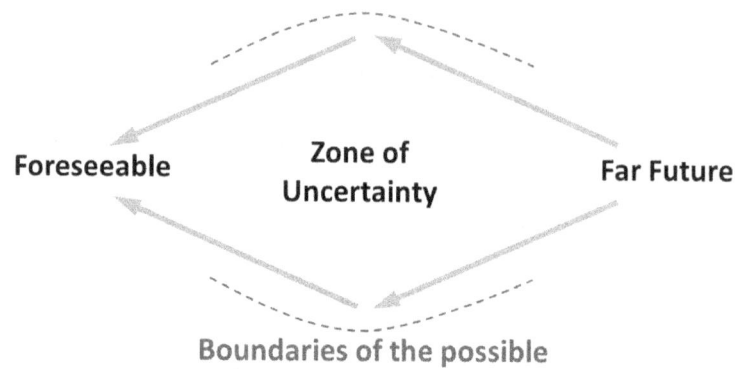

To understand possibilities in the Zone of Uncertainty, first understand the space. What are the boundaries of the possible? I.e. what's impossible? What constraints are there, and what constraints can we create? Then develop scenarios. Conventional planning is closed; scenarios are open. There is no need to decide a plan until we get close. Decide (and execute) at the last responsible moment. Early decisions are waste: work goes stale when the world changes.

Build a portfolio of as many possible scenarios as you can identify, then figure out the potential consequences, and prepare options in response to them. There are an infinite number of scenarios but not so many consequences, so we prepare options for those, creating a corresponding portfolio of options. More on this below.

Other approaches are possible other than scenario analysis, such as future backwards[29], or premortems. What matters is that we come up with that portfolio of possible options which we can start preparing now.

---

[29] https://cynefin.io/wiki/Future_backwards

> What is the value of adhering to a plan that was made at the beginning of a project, when uncertainty was greatest?
>
> – Mark Schwartz, *Seat at the Table*
>
> Predicting the future can only get you into trouble. The task is to manage what is there and to work to create what could [scenarios] and should [vision] be.
>
> – Peter Drucker, 1980
>
> "the traditional ways of planning are outdated. We sense every hour, every day, every week, and react to it."
>
> – Fernando Gonzalez, CEO Cemex

Planning is waste.

Here is a thought experiment for you. Some of the more radical thinkers say we should optimise only for now. Do gap analysis only on your current needs, problems, and risks, not future ones. The theory is that you will then automatically follow a best-possible path because you closely track reality. This may seem crazy but I can't fault the logic. Even if we can't quite cope with that much letting go of the future, it's an insight. And it may be a glimpse of that future.

Here's another thought experiment. A corollary to the logic of "plan for now" is that planning for the future is, in some way, waste.

No plan survives the first encounter with reality. With every step you take, you uncover new information. To a greater or lesser extent, new information modifies or even invalidates your planning. As we said, "Plans are expendable, but planning is essential". What that means is that, even though the result won't last long, the process of putting it together makes you think about all the possibilities. But that can quickly turn into over-investing, into wasted effort. There are better ways. Distinguish between laying out steps and scenario analysis. Thinking about possibilities isn't planning as TU means it. It would be more efficient to admit that most conventional planning is waste, especially investment in plan artefacts, and just do the thinking about scenarios.

So what of all the plans we do now? Why do we do them? Much of it is theatre. It is an illusion to give us comfort that we appear to be in control, that we have some certainty as a foundation on which we can build, some path to go forward. That we know what we are doing. This feels nice, but it's a waste of effort and a misleading delusion. I often say to clients "I'll make up a roadmap if it makes you feel better". Many times, one writes plans so that we will be given funds to do some work. Planning is a little dance we do to get money.

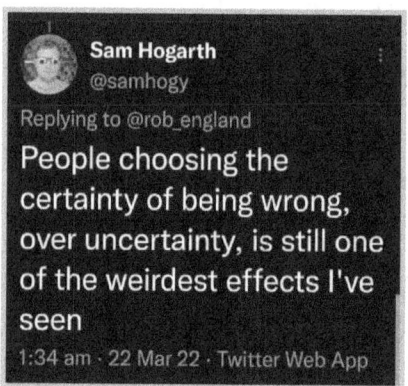

When Cherry explained to clients that the Māori people say the future is behind us and one looks to the past in front, that made one CEO of a corporation annoyed at himself. He had devoted his whole life to central planning. "It means whatever I've done in the past is all wrong because I always plan for 5 years, or at least 1 year. I feel so angry. When I look back, we lost a lot of money by planning, and we missed a lot of opportunities by doing so."

Another motivator to planning is reduction of risk. The idea is that we should *plan to not fail*. What we need to realise is that planning the future is not the most effective way to reduce the risk of the future. Too much happens that we didn't foresee in our plan, and too much information emerges that we don't currently know when we plan. There are better ways to reduce risk. For example:

- Know how you currently function. Use sense-making to understand as much as possible about the current situation.

- Be agile: iterate, increment, experiment, explore.

- Build resilience to cope with the unexpected.

- Create safe-to-fail containment constraints (a concept from Cynefin[30]) for changes.

- Simplify. Do less things. Do things less.

- Defer decisions and work, until the last responsible moment.

Another thing we need to realise is that zero risk is impossible. You can't mitigate a risk away completely. It is entirely possible that a seemingly mundane action will start a chain of events that destroys the organisation. Ask Knight Capital[31]. Failure happens the same way as success: in a complex system you can do the same thing twice and get different results. The tiniest difference in initial conditions leads to wildly different outcomes[32]. The only way to have zero risk is to not do anything ever (the bureaucrat's solution). And that creates new risks of its own.

But wait, there's more. Failure isn't bad anyway. It happens all the time. In fact, it's a normal part of work. Since we don't know the outcome until we do something, then all work is experiment. And in experiments, we will fail sometimes. Failure is an indicator that we are thinking, trying, advancing. Success is found under a pile of failure. Lack of failure should be more cause for worry[33] than presence of failure.

---

[30] Cynefin is a model for understanding (sense-making) situations in complex systems (i.e. the real world). The shift from linear thinking to complex thinking is hard, but all of society needs to do it, and soon. TU have a page about Cynefinhttps://tealunicorn.com/cynefin-3d-updated/. Cynefin originates here https://thecynefin.co/. There is more about this in our other books.
[31] https://www.henricodolfing.com/2019/06/project-failure-case-study-knight-capital.html
[32] The double pendulum illustrates this https://www.youtube.com/watch?v=yWjrnExj-Lg.

The two keys to valuable failure are a learning culture, to capitalise on it, and resilience, to survive it. In a learning organisation, failure is an asset not a cost.

So if we don't plan, what do we do?

To survive and thrive, we do much less conventional planning - what we are going to do, when we are going to do it by, and what will be the measurable outcomes - and more Open Planning.

In a conventional world, we plan short, medium, and long term. VUCA drives a wedge of uncertainty between the short and long term. The more VUCA the world, the wider the gap, so the shorter the short-term planning and the further out the long-term. At Teal Unicorn, pre-cancer-and-COVID we were planning the next year and visioning 2-3 years out. Now we plan[34] only the next 1-3 months, and envision 3-5 years away.

So don't overinvest. Do Open Planning. Plan enough to do just enough to learn enough to revise (or invalidate) the plan. Continue/adjust/abandon/pivot on every iteration. Do minimum viable planning: outcome or goal-based roadmaps, not feature-based roadmaps; stories fleshed out just in time; decisions and work deferred as long as reasonable.

---

[33] https://charleslambdin.wordpress.com/2021/01/14/revisiting-intelligent-failure/amp/
[34] http://tealunicorn.com/planning-horizons-in-a-vuca-world/

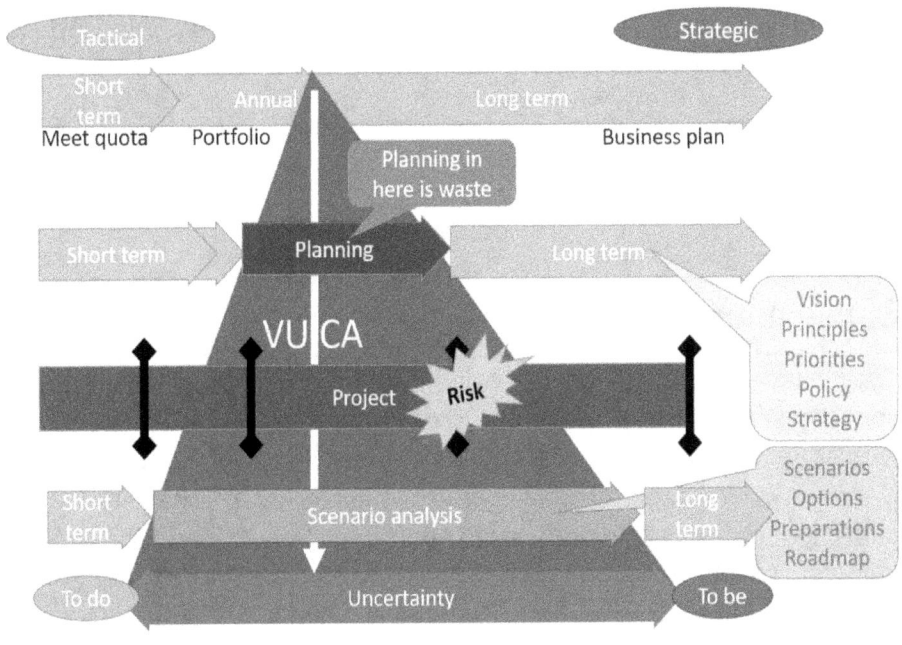

Foreseeable   Zone of Uncertainty   Far Future

(Author's note: So many people have told me that this graphic is too ugly, that I'm now keeping it just to be pig-headed.)

Plan n cycles in the short term.

We can do conventional planning for as many cycles into the future as we can reasonably foresee, the Foreseeable. "Cycles" might be "n" weeks or months or quarters, depending on context, where n is a very small integer. There is a reason why quarterly planning is becoming more popular, rather than annual. And why Scrum is increasingly popular, replanning work on a cadence measured in weeks.

TU uses the analogy of driving on a highway in fog. How far ahead *in time* you can see, measured in seconds, is a function of (a) how fast you are going (b) how thick the fog is and (c) how good your headlights are.

How we plan could be anything from Toyota Improvement Kata to Scaled Agile Framework. TU likes using big-room days - what we call

Community Collaboration - to plan an iteration. We use Open Space Technology or our own patterns for the ritual.

Start where you are. Get a deeper understanding of how your value network actually works.

Sense-making

> "The pace of change in our world is increasing exponentially, but sensemaking — a necessary tool to navigate these turbulent waters — is unseen, undervalued, and underdeveloped. Not only do leaders fail to properly use sensemaking themselves, but it's a capability that is often ignored when hiring, evaluating, developing, and promoting leaders. As a result, leaders and organizations aren't nearly as effective as they could be."
>
> MIT Sloan[35]

Understand as much as possible about your current situation and environment. Use sense-making to cope with the uncertainty and ambiguity. Research shows that sense-making is a predictor of leadership success. It is an essential skill in a VUCA world.

Sensemaking is a big domain. In essence, we create a plausible understanding of the complexity around us, and then test that understanding to refine it or, if necessary, abandon it and start over. Learn, map, test. We:
1. Learn, by bringing together has many and as diverse views as you can
2. Map what you learn, in the broadest sense of mapping through objects, stories and graphics.
3. Experiment to validate your learnings.

---

[35] https://sloanreview.mit.edu/article/the-overlooked-key-to-leading-through-chaos/amp/

Optimise for now. Be steered by your vision (see below) to bias your choices, but respond to immediate needs, problems, and risks, not imagined future ones. The necessity for resilience seems to contradict this, as we build future resilience capability, but the need is immediate even if the work stretches out in time. It's a polarity tension that we just have to work within.

Choose a target state that is SMART (specific, measurable, achievable, relevant, time-bound) or FAST[36] (frequently discussed, ambitious, specific, transparent). Evolution gives us the concept of an "adjacent possible". It must be within the future that we can foresee with high levels of confidence, which isn't much.

Avoid big works. Projects push us into the uncertainty zone. Break them up as much as possible. Iterate, increment, experiment, explore. Reduce risk with short steps so that we stay out of the VUCA zone.

Shift the mindset of your organisation to product not project. Build around long lived products not transitory projects. This allows change to be in a stream not lumps.

All advance involves risk (so does doing nothing). We must mitigate that risk (minimise blast radius):

- Take many small steps.
- Prioritise quickly and simply. If you can't quickly agree on priority, *prioritise that which can be done*: pick something you agree should be easy, and do that. You will learn more, so maybe on the next iteration you can prioritise. At least you will get something done instead of debating.
- Iterate through the steps, repeating a pattern of experiment → observe → learn.
- Expect failure. Prepare for failure. Use pre-mortems.
- Create containment constraints to protect the organisation.
- Respect all constraints. Identify the current bounds and constraints that apply now. What limits should be taken as

---

[36] https://sloanreview.mit.edu/article/with-goals-fast-beats-smart/

given and worked within? Work is the art of the possible. Go where progress is easy.
- Test constraints. Try to find ways through them or ways to move them, if it helps.
- Decide at the last responsible moment. Act at the last responsible moment. Anything premature increases risk and waste. New information comes in. Things change. Work goes stale. You could employ Real Options theory[37].
- Explore your way forward together. The future is darkness. Collaborate to illuminate.

Repeat

This is pure Toyota Kata: once we reach our n-cycles Foreseeable planning horizon, replan. …if not earlier, in response to changing circumstances (new information or external conditions).

Reflect on every repetition. Use a feedback loop, back to design thinking from agile working, to adapt and adjust what we are doing.

Vision n years out.

In a VUCA world, we push visioning further out, we set goals further away, we expand our Far Future horizon. This gives us more room to respond to the world, to be agile. Near-term goals cramp us: they force us to fixed paths and death marches.

When it comes to creating visions, recall that *who* we want to be is much easier to think about than *what* we want to be doing or *where* we want to be. Those things are almost impossible to predict.

Start with where we have come from. As mentioned, the Māori people see the past before them and the future behind them. You can't see the future coming but you can see what has passed. Consider the story that led to where your organisation is now. Tell each other that story. It exposes so much about who you think you are and who you aspire to be.

---

[37] https://www.infoq.com/articles/real-options-enhance-agility/

Honour the legacy: they made many of those decisions for good reasons. Understand what is good about the past, and what you need to let go of. Tradition is both strength and weakness.

Now imagine what a good day at work looks like. We are still not trying to see the future so much as visualise an ideal now.

- How would we know we are successful? Perhaps: we are the first choice; or we can't count how many people we have helped; or we've done something nobody else could …

- What would feel good? Fun. Challenge. Winning. Thanks. Making a difference. Camaraderie. Freedom. Wealth.

- What kind of thing would we like to be doing? Helping the downtrodden. Changing medicine. Pioneering the deep sea. Funding industry. Making things people want. Spreading beauty. Building great things. Making travel safe. Improving working conditions. Advancing technology, or medicine, or science.

Simplify. Don't try to be or do or pursue too many things. Find the essential, the essence of what your organisation represents, what makes it special to you all. That speciality is what will define the organisation: give it a niche, a purpose, and an advantage.

That vision of yourselves guides the next step: scenario analysis. The vision is your navigational star in the distance, not somewhere you want to be in a foreseeable future (especially since we just agreed that we can foresee only a very short time ahead.)

We can then use that vision to imply principles, and from them derive policy and some goals. Instead of one navigational star we have a constellation. "North Star" or "Pole Star" never resonated for we folk in the Southern Hemisphere anyway. At Teal Unicorn, we use Matariki, the Māori name for the Pleiades / the Seven Sisters / Subaru - multiple stars, not one. Our guiding principles and goals are our matariki.

Have a strategic "radar", a way of detecting changes in your sector and your environment. Use these to consider the main things your organisation does, and decide how to respond. That's the essence of strategy. A good pattern is MAD[38]:

1. Magnitude: do it more
2. Activity: do it differently
3. Direction: do something different

Finally, our vision might include some big bets we are taking on where the future is going, e.g.:

- Banks will be disintermediated from retail money; or banks will dominate blockchain.
- The Metaverse is the land of opportunity; or it's another Second Life.
- Pharmaceuticals are set to explode with new science; or the patent monopolies will be smashed.
- Travel will go into decline as we retreat into a virtual world; or travel will boom as we long for reality.
- Space tourism will be huge; or travel to outer space will be banned until it can be carbonless.
- Solar power will grow even bigger; or fusion will render it irrelevant.
- The internet can be monetised; or the internet will drive social revolution.
- Food will be more local and organic; or food will be even more industrialised and synthetic.
- High density living will boom in hostile climates; or people will flee the cities to work remotely.

We call them big bets because they are: you're betting the survival of the organisation on the belief that you are psychic.

You may find the IFF's Three Horizons Model[39] illuminating: business as usual, currently rising innovation, and future innovation that seems

---

[38] https://sloanreview.mit.edu/article/the-essence-of-strategy-is-now-how-to-change/amp/

[39] https://www.internationalfuturesforum.com/three-horizons

unlikely now. (This is not the same model as TU's Foreseeable / Zone of Uncertainty / Far Future).

Or a useful technique of ours is to set "crazy goals". Propose something ambitiously advanced, that seems crazy, that people say is impossible. Don't be constrained by any boundaries you have determined. Then challenge them with that wonderfully powerful hanging question "Impossible unless…??" Use the answers to deconstruct the goal into prerequisites. If they say those prerequisites are in turn "impossible", repeat the process until you work your way back to something that we agree is achievable. Begin there. At a client of ours, a generally conservative manager wanted to encourage new thinking, so he unexpectedly announced a desire to do away with a major change control that he owned. The reaction was shock that it came from him and consternation over the implications. However, it triggered discussion over what first steps could be taken, and opened the group to new possibilities.

Matt Mansell · 1st
Director | Board Chairman | T…
2d

I like the "strategy is a bet, nothing more". I like to say all strategy is wrong. What i mean is that it is a hypothesis about the future that's wrong until proven right. Working towards the strategy is testing the hypotheses.

If your strategy is a 100% correct, it's a description of where you are.

TU don't disagree with much of the book *Humanocracy*, but "…if your organisation doesn't have a unique point of view about the future, then it doesn't have a strategy" is wrong. There are many millions of organisations. It's hard to see how they could all have a unique vision. It's OK to have a similar vision to others. Executing better has been a successful strategy since forever. In VUCA times, being more adaptable is another winning strategy. Being more enlightened is another[40].

Besides, the conventional way of making strategy is often top-down, so staff don't always understand why and what they need to do. Reality and strategy don't align with each other. Many organisations develop their strategy once a year and rarely make adjustments along the way. Our customers often complain that their employees are not delivering on strategic goals.

We advise them to do it differently. Specifically, we use open management methods such as Open Space Technology or our own Collaborative Community Rituals to develop strategic plans. Instead of a top-down decision, we invite everyone in the organisation to participate in strategy planning. After one event, the Head of Retail of a large bank said to Cherry: "It's unbelievable, it normally takes us at least three months to do the strategy. All departments submit their own strategy, then we adjust it to become a general strategy. Even though it took so much time and effort, we still didn't have a good overall picture like we got here in one day".

A CEO of a financial company said: "I always thought my staff were not knowledgeable enough to participate in strategy making, but after today I think differently. It turns out that they have many great ideas, more realistic ideas and initiatives than senior executives. We observed what was going on and were amazed. When everyone built strategies together, came up with solutions, they produced amazing results."

There is a client of ours that was a little lost: they didn't know their goal, purpose, what they exist for. Staff would do as told without understanding why, and what they are supposed to do. They have now been going for three years but had no idea about anything, so people could come to the job without knowing or understanding. Cherry said to the CEO "A week from now, we can do one workshop to make sure everything's clear. We can do planning for the future,

---

[40] Read TU's book *Open Management*

what you really want to focus on, and what products you want to deliver". Cherry spent one day with all the staff, about fifty. They are mostly smart youngsters. She brought them together doing an obeya wall, visualising from the value idea to delivery and then improvement. In one day they created almost everything, from the big picture of the value and purpose to the value stream of functions, the products they saw as strategic and what to focus on, and then the tasks, and then kanban, along with a map of current skills (TU use Shu-Ha-Ri), a skills marketplace, and a development programme. The Miro board they created that day continues to be their central work visualisation and planning. Their business is e-learning, so they have some great designers who created the board for Cherry as the day went along.

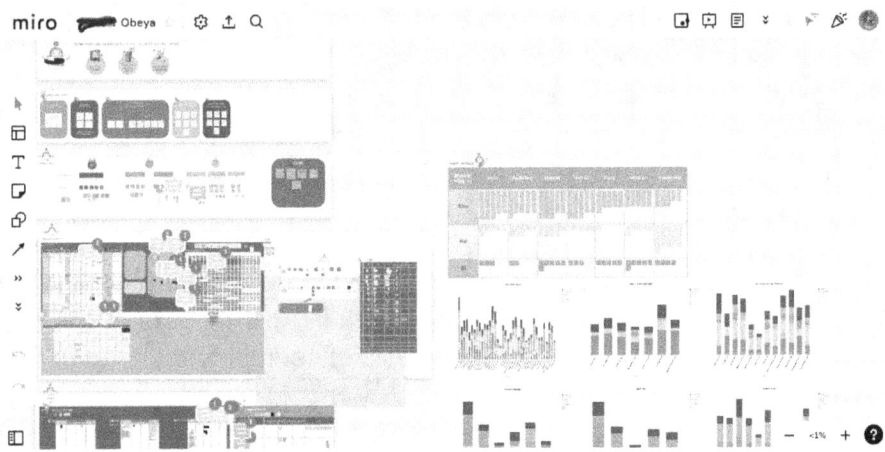

The CEO said "I didn't have anything to do, I added nothing to this. I just see everything up in front of me even better than what I can imagine of my organisation". The best part of the story is that Cherry had no idea how the day would happen, going into the event. She allows the days to be emergent, to shape them as they play out.

Scenario analysis

In between planning (the Foreseeable) and visioning (the Far Future) is the wide Zone of Uncertainty. In that zone, the future is unknowable; and the behaviour of the complex system is unpredictable.

We can begin by understanding the space that we are exploring, as best we can. Although we cannot know what will happen within the space, we can define that which is probably impossible in the time before the Far Future - it is outside the space. E.g, replacing all our factories; expanding into Russia; fusion power. We can even create constraints for ourselves to say we will not go outside that space. For example, when I (Rob) first started seeking my fortune on the internet, I ruled out crime, spam, or porn. (It turns out there aren't many other money-making options.) These voluntary constraints can be things we won't do; or they can also be choices, things we have chosen not to do as part of our strategy.

To explore this space, we should understand scenarios, consequences, and options, and the mapping between them (see next section). Scenarios allow us to think about the possible, and expand our minds to those possibilities. Consequences are the likely outcomes of those scenarios. Options are a hand of cards we assemble, to play as we need them in response to consequences that actually arise.

Perhaps the money we save from not doing unnecessary planning will help to pay for the resilience we need in the face of inevitable surprises and failures, and for the multiple experiments required to find a way forward in complexity.

In this book, this discussion is depicted as an either/or model: plan for short term, then scenarios after some cutoff. Of course the world isn't that black and white. There is much grey. The line between Foreseeable and the Zone of Uncertainty isn't crisp. We can usually see some future milestones beyond the foreseeable horizon: near goals we set in the zone, or scenarios that have such a high probability that we better plan for them. Often we need to plan much further ahead than we feel comfortable (more on that below). Conversely, we may be in such uncertain times that we can only think of scenarios for the present, and plan for nothing.

Note that "scenario" can be used in multiple ways, e.g. to refer to customer persona journeys in user interface design. I don't mean that. I mean future business scenarios. Also "scenarios" are used to describe a far future. I don't mean that either. In our context, scenario analysis fills the gap, the Zone of Uncertainty, between short term planning as far as we can see, which isn't very far – a few months, the Foreseeable; and far out visions, which are years away (you might like to use scenarios for visioning too), the Far Future.

The Teal Unicorn approach:

1. Define your constraints. View them as enabling not disabling. Challenge them every time.

2. Build a portfolio of as many possible scenarios as you can identify.

3. Identify what the consequences would be. A smaller number of consequences will result from our scenarios, as some scenarios may lead to the same outcomes, so consequences are a simpler list to deal with.

4. Identify options to respond to the consequences. Again, an option may respond to multiple consequences, so hopefully the list gets shorter still.

5. Start work now on preparing options where you can.

6. Repeat 1-5 at least annually; quarterly for some. Trigger an immediate cycle if a significant scenario emerges – have some sort of regular strategic radar analysis to detect it (one would like to think this already exists in your organisation).

Don't be technically fastidious about this analysis. It doesn't have to be perfect or exhaustive. We are dealing with a VUCA world, foggy and constantly shifting. So we can over-invest in this analysis just as we can over-invest in planning. The descriptions of scenarios that seem closer or more probable can be clear and fine; the others can be vague and coarse.

Scenarios

In some scenario modelling, it's about numerical probabilities. TU believes that's overthinking. The probability estimates are always pulled out of an orifice. We don't know.

Other scenario modelling approaches aren't really dealing with scenarios at all: they try to describe what "should" happen. That's fortune telling. Scenarios are what might happen.

Diverge then converge. First we generate as many scenarios as we can within the space of possibility, then we focus on the most important (not the same as most likely, though there is of course overlap). We will have a set of scenarios from the last time we did this, because we will do it regularly. Put them aside for now, and imagine afresh. Starting with a prior list stifles thinking. Ensure a diverse group is thinking about it. Make it management-light (or at least proportionate to their overall numbers). If conventional people are startled by those participating, you've got it about right. Interns. The Board. The oldest staff. Vocal critics. From other business divisions. Suppliers. Ex-employees. Industry analysts. Competitors. The gardening staff. Someone's kids.

Use all sorts of approaches to generate scenarios, to stimulate ideas.

- We can use Open Space Technology and other workshop techniques: Future Backwards, pre-mortems, role plays, hypotheticals, red teams…
- Tell stories. Imagine a time traveller from the future reporting back. Narrative stimulates creativity.
- Understand what your bounds are, both the bounds of possibility and the constraints that you set yourself. Constraints don't limit our thinking: they simplify, and stimulate us to look in innovative directions. Use your strategic radar to identify incoming influences.
- Do a PESTLEE analysis (Political, Economic, Social, Technological, Legal, Environmental, Ethical).
- Look for these types of scenarios[41]:

1. Evolution: all trends continue as expected. Things gently move toward a predictable end point. As we said, this is unlikely, but it provides a data point.
2. Revolution: a new disruptive factor fundamentally changes the situation.
3. Cycles: what goes around comes around. Boom follows bust follows boom follows bust.
4. Infinite Expansion: exciting trends continue. Think of the computer industry in the 1950s.
5. Lone Ranger: the triumph of the lone hero against the forces of inertia.
6. My Generation: changes in culture and demographics affect the situation.
7. The Infinite Game[42]: change the rules to benefit all stakeholders.
8. The Null Hypothesis: nothing changes in the world
9. Option Zero: we do nothing, just coast.
10. The Ghost Scenario[43]

> Our prevailing narrative, whatever it is, frames the situation for us. This is sometimes called the "ghost scenario." If scenarios are stories about the future, the ghost scenario is the assumed future in which the existing strategy would be successful; but it's only one of many possible futures. There is always then at least one ghost scenario, replete with its underlying — and typically unaccounted for — assumptions.
> – Charles Lambdin

11. The Black Swan: the outcome that never even occurred to us to imagine - that isn't in our scenario analysis anywhere; the unexpected.

---

[41] Some come from The Art of the Long View by Peter Schwartz. © 1991 Peter Schwartz http://mybook.to/Art-Long-View

[42] http://www.infinite-game.net/beginnersguide

[43] https://charleslambdin.com/2020/04/07/strategy-and-ghost-stories/amp/

12. Total catastrophe: planning for a Zombie Apocalypse is fun, funny, and at the same time enlightening, to think about what to do when things are going ridiculously badly.

Try to overcome cognitive bias, comfort zones, and blind spots. Some important cognitive biases are[44]:

- Availability: sources of information that are easily accessible or top of mind.
- Probability neglect: overestimate the importance of low-probability events.
- ...and conversely Overconfidence: risks and uncertainties discounted.
- Stability: assume that the future will resemble the past.
- Social: groupthink inhibits open discussion.
- Sunflower: subordinates defer to the boss.
- Anchoring: once we say a number, all subsequent numbers will seem high or low relative to it.

Be aware that trend-extrapolation is usually wrong: the world isn't that simple or predictable, it doesn't follow simple graph lines.

Once we have as many scenarios as possible, only then check against the previous list and decide which ones to carry over, which ones we missed this time, and which ones are no longer possible. (Note: not which ones are no longer likely. We consider all scenarios.)

> "scenarios are not predictions but can provide a deeper foundation of knowledge and self-awareness in approaching the future" [45]

Unpack the scenarios with tools such as:

---

[44] *Overcoming obstacles to effective scenario planning*, Drew Erdmann, Bernardo Sichel, and Luk Yeung https://www.mckinsey.com/business-functions/strategy-and-corporate-finance/our-insights/overcoming-obstacles-to-effective-scenario-planning

[45] *Living in the Futures,* Angela Wilkinson and Roland Kupers hbr.org/2013/05/living-in-the-futures

- Four quadrant matrices of all sorts, (enhance with a third dimension as bubbles) e.g.
    - Likelihood-Impact
    - Impact-Uncertainty
- Heat maps
- Framing it in different ways ("10% fat" vs "90% fat-free")
- Wardley Maps

Reject certainty, surface the uncertainties, look for cognitive biases, and identify assumptions.

Unravel multiple factors. People tend to think a conjunction of factors is more likely than individually[46]. Peel them apart and consider the separate scenarios.

Once we have generated scenarios, then some folk like to rank their priority for our attention, probably by an index based on both likelihood (probability, plausibility) and impact (risk: ethical, financial, operational, reputational, compliance/legal). But we should still try to consider them all. It's not about selecting a few to work on.

Consequences

As part of developing scenarios, recognise/infer/deduce/model the consequences, good and bad. Develop a new list/portfolio of consequences and link consequences to scenarios. Usually multiple scenarios map to a single consequence: there are less consequences than there are scenarios. For example, COVID locked everybody at home, so they couldn't work in the office. A murder in the lift lobby of your building will have the same consequence.

Again there are many tools to consider consequences, including:

- FMEA: Failure Mode and Effects Analysis
- Six Thinking Hats

---

[46] *Scenario Planning: A Tool for Strategic Thinking,* Paul J.H. Schoemaker https://sloanreview.mit.edu/article/scenario-planning-a-tool-for-strategic-thinking/

- Pre-mortems

Options

Conduct more exercises to identify as many of our future options as possible for responding to consequences. They're not one-option-for-one-consequence. Map out the many-to-many relationship between consequences and the potential options to respond to them. Options are similar to contingency plans, though broader. Contingency implies a crisis, which is only one kind of consequence. Options are considered responses to all sorts of consequences, good and bad. Some options will be defensive/resilient, some will be assertive/opportunistic.

One of the blockers to generating options is to see consequences as devastating. We need to understand the impacts of a consequence as enabling constraints that guide us in finding options. It is what it is. If a consequence presents us with a dilemma, an irreconcilable conflict of priorities, we need to accept the polarity tension and adopt "yes/and" thinking to move forward. A dilemma is an enabling constraint.

There are documented techniques for moving forward from an apparent impasse to find options. Negotiators do it. Problem solvers do it. Techniques include[47]:

- Mapping the win-lose and lose-win in order to deduce the win-win outcome.
- Deconstructing the reasoning that led us to a binary dilemma to identify places we could have branched to other possibilities.
- Ensuring we are inclusive of cognitive and social diversity to find as creative and innovative options as possible.

We want to build a set of options like a hand of cards, which we can play when the opportunity presents itself, usually in response to one of our consequences coming true, or something like it.

---

[47] https://www.strategy-business.com/blog/Five-ways-to-avoid-the-pitfalls-of-binary-decisions

Options attempt to *influence, avoid, prepare for, and/or exploit* consequences. We can test the completeness of our options for each consequence by checking each of those four categories.

Rank the options by priority for our attention. E.g. value the options. (Not by how much we like them. It is what it is). Real Options[48] is much in vogue to assess the value, instead of discounted cash flows, but a hybrid is better[49]. Real Options are alternatives or choices that may be available for the business when appraising work items. When a decision maker has the right (but no obligation) to take a specific action, we say the option exists.

Modularity of systems also creates options:

> *When the design of an artefact is "modularized," the elements of the design are split up and assigned to modules according to a formal architecture or plan. Some of the modules are "hidden," meaning that design decisions in those modules do not affect decisions in other modules; some of the modules are "visible," meaning that they embody "design rules" that hidden-module designers must obey if the modules are to work together. Modular designs offer alternatives that non-modular ("interdependent") designs do not provide. Specifically, in the hidden modules, designers may replace early, inferior solutions with later, superior solutions. Such alternatives can be modeled as "real options." In Design Rules, Volume 1: The Power of Modularity (MIT Press, 2000) we sought to categorize the major options implicit in a modular design, and to explain how each type can be valued in accordance with modern finance theory. ... an example [is] the valuation of the modular options "splitting" and "substitution." We show that the key drivers of the "net option value" of a particular module are (1) its "technical potential" (labeled s, because it operates like volatility in financial option theory); (2) the cost of mounting independent design experiments; and (3) the "visibility" of the*

---

[48] https://www.kanbanmaturitymodel.com/2020/09/01/real-options-more-than-deferring-commitment/
[49] http://hbr.org/2004/12/making-real-options-really-work

module in question. The option value of a system of modules in turn can be approximated by adding up the net option values inherent in each module and subtracting the cost of creating the modular architecture. A positive value in this calculation justifies investment in a new modular architecture. [50]

Over time we will start recognising generic options that can become part of regular work to always be preparing them.

Mapping

The resulting lists of scenarios, consequences, and options, and the mapping between them, is our scenario map.

Visualise the map in multiple ways. Put the smart kids on this task. E.g.

- bubble charts for multidimensional views of the scenario portfolio
- causal analysis: herringbone charts, causal state/loop diagrams for each scenario (and how they may be inter-related)
- strategic radar or timeline
- relationship maps of which options relate to which scenarios
- Wardley Maps
- overlaid on other models e.g. Cynefin
- a narrative landscape drawing as a visual depiction

Stories

Select a small number of representative scenarios to try to reflect the whole portfolio. Build them out into compelling stories to help stakeholders engage with the future.

---

[50] *The Option Value of Modularity in Design*, Clark and Baldwyn, May 2002 SSRN Electronic Journal

Actions

The final step is to draw up a list of actions we can take now to start preparing for each and every option, and add these to our backlog(s) for prioritisation with other work. E.g.

- Research
- Experiment
- Reduce risks
- Build resilience
- Stockpile
- Prepare to exploit

It is smart to invest now in groundwork for many of the options. We want to get off to the best possible start if an option gets invoked/enacted.

Here are some other considerations for Open Planning:

---

[51] https://poorlydrawnlines.com/

Goals

People and organisations will always want to set goals. It is natural to give ourselves outcomes to strive for. We see moves that would be strategically impactful if we could achieve them. We see survival options that we really need to put in place. There is stuff we feel we have to get done.

It's not wrong to have goals. It is how we treat our goals that matter. They are a beacon on a hill instead of a star in the sky - they're closer. They give us a direction (which should align with our distant visions) and we can actually get there within a foreseeable time. Just like a navigational star they don't prescribe a specific direction or set of steps; they are just an influence on our planning. We must review constantly and be prepared to abandon them and switch to a different guiding beacon - extinguish that one and find a different hill.

Projects

When it comes to the tangible non-fungible world of physical objects that are built once, or big changes to highly complicated abstract systems, sometimes the time-span of planning has to be longer, intruding into the Zone of Uncertainty. Let's collectively call these situations "projects". They are unavoidable. There is a polarity tension between the reality that we cannot plan far into the future, and the reality that we have to. Planning can push into the Zone of Uncertainty. But do it knowingly, and recognise the risks of trying to know the unknowable.

Here are some strategies to help us:

- Make the project management as agile as possible. Many agile practices can be adopted[52] even within the constraints of a fixed project. There is a global movement amongst the project management community to develop this approach.

---

[52] https://kanbanize.com/agile/industries/agile-construction

- Shift the definition of deliverables from defined requirements and specific outputs, to value outcomes for the target stakeholders. How will the experience be different? The closest thing in conventional project planning is the defined benefits.

- Define the outputs in the conventional way only for some early wins in a first phase.

- Wherever possible, keep timelines loose as a roadmap, not committed as milestones.

- Break one big output into subcomponents, as small as possible. Over time, we remove the dependencies between organisational units and technology systems to allow us to break work up smaller.

- Make it as modular as possible, consisting of repeating standardised components.

- Reuse proven solutions as much as possible.

- Find fast techniques. Accelerate learning and feedback. Don't give the world time to change before we build it.

- Find parts of the project that can be done with capital-A Agile, e.g. using Scrum or Kanban methodologies.

- Show how decisions impact future options. Make decisions that keep options as open as possible.

- Make it normal practice that all decisions and plans are deferred until the last responsible moment.

- Use the Last Planner® System[53] where planning evolves iteratively, and the team who are actually going to do the work do the final fully detailed planning.

---

[53] https://leanconstructionblog.com/What-is-the-Last-Planner-System.html

> The choice is not an either/or: scalable or not scalable. It is a matter of degree: getting as much scalability as you can into any project, including the least likely ones.
>
> Bent Flyvbjerg[54]

Direction

People get uncomfortable that lack of planning seems directionless. It is not directionless. We have our long-term vision and our immediate mission to help direct us. We have principles – what Teal Unicorn calls "matariki" or navigational stars – to guide our decision making.

We are free to set goals or outcomes or what the military call "desired effects" within the Zone of Uncertainty, so long as we understand that they are just flags in the ground that can be knocked over at any time. We can have a roadmap if it is disposable and flexible.

And finally – as we have mentioned already – there is a school of thought that there is nothing wrong with being "directionless". Planning and optimising for the present, organically responding to the environment in an optimal way, allows direction to be emergent and adaptive.

Roadmap

A roadmap provides a sense of direction, and reassurance. The fact is that it is unlikely to come true, so we should make minimum investment, but it serves a psychological purpose, and sometimes exposes dependencies. Build outcome- or goal-based roadmaps, not feature-based roadmaps. Show the many decision points and the resultant uncertainty. Don't draw a "happy path".

I have a recurring struggle with clients who want to see a timeline on the roadmap. If I fail to explain why it doesn't have one, I do it just to make them feel better.

---

[54] https://hbr.org/2021/11/make-megaprojects-more-modular

> ...usually when you draw a roadmap the roads are already built. No navigation system could plot a route from here to there when the terrain is shifting as fast as it does under our feet now.
>
> - Alex Kazemi[55]

Control

There is a perception that if we are constantly changing direction, we must be out of control. Actually we are just abandoning the illusion of control. The cruise control on your car does not allow you to lock in the steering direction. You are constantly adjusting direction in response to the external environment. But you still know where you are going. And you are always prepared to adjust your destination in response to circumstances as well, e.g. traffic jams, family emergencies, or a better idea.

---

[55] https://thespinoff.co.nz/society/23-08-2021/if-you-listen-closely-enough-you-can-hear-the-whole-system-shudder/

Better ways to advance our capability

Many say this is the new normal: no normal. You may be doing great or you may be struggling, but one thing is clear: what got you here won't get you there. We flex and writhe to survive and thrive in an unpredictable world.

The organisation (or society) will change as fast as it possibly can, and no faster, and only if the people want to change. If they don't want to, if they are coerced, it will be slower. In a VUCA world where adaptability is survival, this principle isn't just self-evident, it's essential. Only by better ways of managing, that restore humanity to work, can we achieve the speed of change that we need to be agile and resilient, to adapt constantly to the world. People need to do change, not have it done to them.

In one client, they had been talking with TU about having three months planning rather than a year planning like normal. Out of nowhere, the old-school CEO rejected a one-year plan from his staff, saying it is unreasonable to plan so far ahead anymore. People messaged Cherry saying "someone just called your name". Lesson: people don't resist change when it's their own idea.

Growing capability

If people:

- have autonomy, mastery, and purpose
- feel loved and appreciated, feel that the employer is benevolent
- feel safe to fail, to speak up, to share
- feel honestly, fairly paid

...if we have all those things, we don't need carrots or sticks.

Carol Stanford showed TU that such a humanistic view is the first step, that more is needed.

> *We need to each make big promise[s] to enable buyer/beneficiaries' lives with our efforts; so big we have to grow to do so, and active a developmental path, not mastery which stops us; Then we need to learn to operate from external considering, other's purposes, not our own, which has nothing to do with being appreciated and loved, but serving something; and then also develop an internal locus of control worldview, versus victimhood, or blame which is hindered by working on creating a safe place and fair pay as a driver.*[56]

Her book *No More Feedback* has been enlightening. It ties in to everything TU believe and do, and takes us another increment forward in our understanding.

She reminds us to have not just vision but *ambition* for the group ("big promises"). She introduced us to a triad of necessary "capacities" for change: internal locus of control, external considering, and purposeful personal agency (read her book).

> *These are concrete and grounded and can be translated in every action into practice immediately.*

From this, we learned that it is not enough to set people free, to liberate them, to give them authority. We must also allow - and help - them to develop the capacities to make the most of that freedom.

We must also bring them back to conversations that apply these abstract principles in real immediate contexts, to drive continual improvement. If I were to distil her whole book *No More Feedback* in a simple sentence it would be: stop telling people how to be better and start asking them how it could be better[57].

Many years ago, Marcus Buckingham taught me, in *First Break All the Rules*, to build on people's strengths, not their weaknesses. We should

---

[56] Discussion with the author on LinkedIn
[57] How ironic that I learned this from her feedback online

set them free to find their place in the system where they excel, and to pursue their own personal ambitions to contribute more.

What I (Rob) often have to check myself on is idealising people, expecting too much too soon. People blossom, but only at a human rate of change, and only as far as their current capability. We must allow time for them to change and grow.

Moreover, nobody is excellent at everything. If you have to recruit superstars to make your system succeed, it's a bad system. A good system of work succeeds with ordinary people, with an assortment of strengths and weaknesses. We collaborate, we team, we compensate for each other. Together we are better than apart - that's the very reason organisations exist.

Therefore, don't design operating models for perfect people. Assume human error, weakness, suboptimal performance, corruption, and even malice. Build in checks and balances to track functioning of the system. This is about informational feedback, not personal feedback to individuals. To allow people to succeed, we provide them transparency of work (what is happening, who is doing it, how is it going), collaboration to give them a way to contribute, and support for their personal growth.

This support is what HR should be there for. People need coaching, mentoring, training, immersion, community, and mobility to develop and change their own "job description".

There is a growing realisation in business that - for decades - we have shut down the business practice of growing good people within the organisation. In the name of Friedmanism, development of people was cut back or eliminated, and we sought to hire people already expert, presumably developed by somebody else. The consequence has been ageing and scarce expertise. At last, we are seeing a return to hiring staff to grow into the work required of them.

Advancing the system of work

We need ways of advancing (TU don't like the word "transform": it implies magic, external agency, and step-change) which arise from the people, done by them not to them.

Here is an idealised approach which Teal Unicorn might use with a client. Of course the reality will be entirely different. We won't know what it is until we do. Only by exploring with the client do we uncover the specific activities required. The journey we follow then emerges - it is not planned (of course).

1 Get started

In this order (ideally):

1. Visualise work. Put activity on a wall (or a virtual one). Start to get a picture of where the issues are.

2. Communicate. Get together. Develop mutual respect for each others' challenges and needs.

3. Create some headroom to start improvement, with initial tactics to get some breathing space. If people are 100% busy (or more), nothing is ever going to improve until you prioritise improving work over doing work. This is cold hard logic. Don't move on until the concept of slack[58] is accepted by all who control workload.

4. No, really. Don't move on until there is headroom for improvements. Otherwise you're all just dreaming.

5. Explore the delivery value stream(s) together. Take managers to the gemba[59], to where the work is done. Develop a common understanding of value flow, where the bottlenecks are (Theory of Constraints view), and where the overburden, inconsistencies, and waste are (Lean view).

---

[58] Read *Slack*, Tom DeMarco
[59] https://tealunicorn.com/going-to-the-gemba/

6. Have you created that headroom yet?

7. Visualise flow of work. Develop a common view of the value stream. Value Stream Mapping may produce the first-ever holistic view of the work. Usually, at least one senior person is shocked by how it really works.

8. Wait for the pennies to drop: management will see places where they are part of the problem (see the first half of John Seddon's recent book *Beyond Command and Control*). Ask management to find ways to get out of the way of flow. These are low hanging fruit, and very good for morale.

9. Broker a common set of principles for everyone to work by, at least within the scope of our control. Who are we? Who do we want to be? What do we stand for? How do we do things around here? TU have a long list of examples[60].

10. Go long on vision. Strategy and goals need to be far enough out to provide direction through all the intervening VUCA, leaving enough room for agility. Build a consensus around vision, principles, policy. Open Space rituals[61] are good.

11. Introduce and evenly distribute three sets of ideas: better ways of working[62] ("human systems adaptability"), better ways of managing[63] (especially servant leader/manager[64]), and better ways of thinking[65] (teal, humanistics, new age…). This is why foundation training and certification are OK. It creates a baseline of common concepts and language. Some evangelising is good.

---

[60] https://tealunicorn.com/umm/
[61] https://openspaceworld.org/wp2/what-is/
[62] https://tealunicorn.com/nwomaw
[63] https://tealunicorn.com/nwom
[64] https://tealunicorn.com/pull-decisions-up-to-the-closest-level-to-the-work/
[65] https://tealunicorn.com/nwot

2 Manage the backlog.

- In the perfect world, we would have only one backlog for all work to be done: new features, improvements, refactoring, bugs/defects, maintenance, housework. Get as close to this as you can.

- Likewise, we want to have only one backlog for products and your own work systems. I.e. all of the above "new features, improvements…" encompasses both what you deliver and how you deliver it. It's best to include it all in one funnel of work to be done, not multiple conflicting funnels.

- Prioritise for now. But be careful how you interpret "now": don't let it mean that the urgent trumps the important. Work on what is important now. That includes building resilience, and laying groundwork for future options. Address current needs, problems, and risks.

- Always maintain headroom. Spare capacity, "slack", is essential. Focus on creating even more headroom, through:
    - demand management – how to say "not now".
    - backlog prioritisation – how to say "not yet".
    - tighter product management collaboration – how to say "after you".
    - low-hanging fruit of flow optimisation, quick wins.
    - automation of work – typically pays for itself in three iterations if you share it.
    - faster restoration of service after an incident.
    - reduced failure demand[66] – higher quality work.

---

[66] John Seddon talks about user requests being either value demand or failure demand. Failure demand is requests to fix what wasn't done properly the first time. It is a quality issue. All failure demand is waste.

3 Explore the Zone of Uncertainty.

- Push the envelope. Explore the boundaries of your organisation. The edges are interesting. They define the entity. Shifting them changes who we are. Change happens at the margin: the "adjacent possible"[67],

- Grow experimental thinking. Encourage it. Build an experiment programme to promote, track, share, and consolidate experiments. Walk the walk on embracing failure as learning.

- Start scenario analysis and generating options.

- Create small teams to chase options and generate backlog tasks as preparations for options. What can we add to the backlog now to lay the groundwork? What contingencies are needed for survival resilience?

- Roadmap if you must. Show a possible sequence and dependencies but no timeline. Don't waste time on detail that is guesswork.

- Track fixed milestones for informational purposes (and risk management). Don't plan to meet them beyond the Foreseeable short term, unless reality insists. We just don't know.

4 Build resilience.

Resilience Engineering is as important as developing organisational changes. We will fail in our experiments - it is a given. The VUCA world will slap us. S&&t happens. Build a Resilience Engineering capability to improve the odds of our continued survival. I nearly said "ensure" survival. Nobody can do that – there is no Zero Risk. Doing anything creates a risk of catastrophe. So does doing nothing.

---

[67] Stephen Johnson, *Where Good Ideas Come From*

- Grow a community of people who are positive, confident, and mentally strong to deal with challenges and shocks. Help and support those who slip.

- Grow people's capabilities to do what we need to do, as identified by current needs and scenarios. Identify and develop strengths not weaknesses. Do what you're good at.

- Build antifragile systems, and practices to learn from failure.

- Build resilient systems and practices, that absorb shocks with minimum damage, through redundancy, robustness, and recoverability.

- Grow situational awareness. Keep radar on to detect emerging conditions. Build sense-making capabilities using available methods: OODA, Cynefin…

5 Grow organisational agility

…to develop changes quickly and responsively. Plenty has been written about that[68]. Here are some of the main ideas from our book *The agile Manager (small a)*:

- Create an improvement "machine" of people and activities to keep improvement moving.

- Create bubbles of new ways within the broader organisation. Protect them with buffers: white space between them and the rest of the work system. Produce proof points evidence that new ways work.

- Find triads[69] of mutually supporting peers or near-peers.

- Create or wait for an executive mandate, so that we can develop (incubate) an organisation-wide model.

---

[68] We have a reading list here https://tealunicorn.com/tam-reading
[69] from the book *Tribal Leadership*, Logan, Fischer-Wright, and King.

- Once we have a minimum viable version of the new way of working, start an invitational [pull don't push] movement for wider adoption. Run interference on the organisational immune system: watch out for those who see it as their role to protect the organisation from these dangerous new ideas. Feed back to improve our new way of delivery. Use Toyota Kata or similar to develop it.

6 Break down the behaviours that hold you back

E.g.

- *People as a resource*: they're human colleagues, not machines.

- *Expectation of Zero Risk*: risk can never be totally eliminated - we must be always expecting failure.

- *Failure is not an option*: if people do not feel free to fail, they will avoid doing anything.

- *Accountability for goals and KPIs:* the outcome is always unknown, and always beyond the control of those doing the work.

- *"Alpha" command-control management, fear, firing, lack of safety*: in such a culture, people are less productive, and unwilling to act.

- *Change fatigue, cynicism, bitterness, distrust, learned helplessness, bad habits, obstructiveness, corruption*: such "culture debt" puts a drag on any action.

- *Silos, barriers, handoffs, demarcation, fixed roles, isolation, fiefdoms, tribalism*: a lack of collaboration and community reduces flow and productivity.

- *Hierarchy, top down, rarified heights, ignorance of gemba*: management don't know what is really happening or why.

- *Managers are smarter, deference to seniority, HIPPOs*: much human potential and institutional knowledge is wasted.

- *Secrecy, need to know, closed door decision making, suppression of bad news, elephants in the room, theatre*: there is much busywork that achieves nothing.

- *Insular resistance to diversity (e.g. bro culture; nationalism; alignment to a religion)*: reduces creativity, drives people out, and damages morale,

- *Middle management bureaucracy*: reporting overheads, management by numbers, controls that prevent work ... (Don't eliminate middle managers. They can be your most important resource if they're allowed to be.)

7 Grow capability

New ways of managing and working will require new skills in individuals and new capabilities in groups.

- Recruit for a new vision of who you want to be. Hire exemplars (people who show that it is possible, and demonstrate how it is done).

- Protect your people. Offer opportunities to grow into new skills so they can stay with the organisation. They're too valuable to lose. Growing people is coming back into fashion. And it's the decent thing to do.

- Technology, cognitive, collaboration and emotional skills will be paramount. We can grow these now – things like problem solving, insight, team building, resource management and implementation skills.

8 Engineer for adaptability

Recall that adaptability = agility + resilience. Technology plays a role.

- Software tools. On its own, technology solves nothing. Technology makes our advancement more efficient and effective, but without changes to behaviour and systems, tech doesn't create advances. Buy tools to help the work improvements that are going on, not to make them happen.

- Automation. We want to change faster (agility) with less errors (also agility) and less impact on existing systems (resilience). Humans can't do them all manually beyond some ceiling, beyond which speed and quality are traded off with each other. We must automate to go beyond. Here are some points about automation to bear in mind:

  - We can only automate that which is defined and repeatable, i.e. transactional work not knowledge work. In other words, we automate toil, drudge.

  - Automation of work is only of value once that automation is made available to others. If it is held close to those who built it, they are still a bottleneck.

  - Automation is antifragile: we improve it every time we fail.

- Modularity. Over time, we should minimise dependencies through modular architectures, for our systems, our software, our machinery. This increases our ability to change (agility) and reduces failure blast radius (resilience).

9 Measure your wake

Vision forward but measure progress looking back. Don't benchmark against perfect. Benchmark against where you have come from.

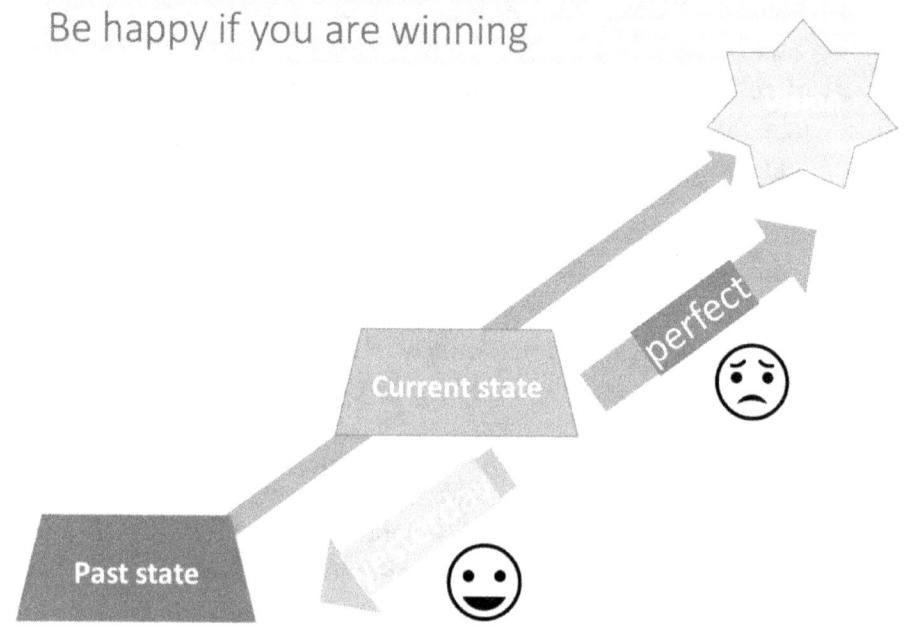

Thriving on adversity and opportunity

"The harder I work the luckier I get." Luck is when preparation meets opportunity.

Once you have done the work to be more adaptable and resilient, then everything our rapidly changing world throws at us can present an opportunity. You can capitalise on the reality we find ourselves in. VUCA is not something anyone can solve, it is a constraint that we turn into a creative one: "Yes, and…". We can thrive.

The risk is that many want to focus on "getting back to normal", "minimising the damage", and "controlling risk". We need to show that there is no going back, the world has changed. Regressing actually embeds the damage and puts us at risk of coming to a halt as we "stabilise".

Build on failure through antifragility.

It's not that failure will necessarily come more in the new world (we are pretty good at failure already), but we will engineer our work so that failure comes in many smaller increments, in safe-to-fail experiments, with minimum blast radius, so that we can maximise learning and minimise damage. As we build our resilience, we will care less about any damage as well. Instead of failure being a terrible cost, it becomes a stream of value. Our systems become designed to grow through failure, not to crumble. Failure has real value if – and only if – we have a learning culture, with continual improvement practices baked in, and antifragile systems that grow stronger under stress.

Respond to disruption of your market

Disruption is much rarer than the analysts, consultants, vendors, and media would have us believe, but it does happen. We can respond in different ways for our own benefit:

- Fight back
- Double down
- Retrench
- Move away

Exploit turbulence to disrupt and open your future.

Sometimes the level of environmental VUCA is beyond our ability to cope with in business-as-usual. The COVID pandemic is of course the classic example. Sometimes our own internal failures are more than we can cope with. There is no such thing as zero risk, and the magnitude of a failure is unpredictable. Catastrophic failure is a possible outcome for every action we take at work, no matter how trivial.

Either way, we can find ourselves in a chaotic situation which is beyond our ability to understand or even observe. When circumstances are beyond our ability to manage, our first response must be to act. Our first act should be to introduce constraints, to try to reduce the chaos. Then we can observe what the result was, and adjust accordingly. As we constrain the system, we try to move to a different situation, based on what limited information we have, what limited reasoning we can do, and what instincts tell our most experienced people who have been dancing with the system.

For those who want a much more advanced guide to responding to chaos, the EU has published (free) the paper *Managing complexity (and chaos) in times of crisis*[70], a field guide for decision makers inspired by the Cynefin framework. Don't expect a light read – TU are still absorbing it.

So anything that throws us into disruptive turbulence is an opportunity to try new things, to start with a clean slate, to rethink how we work. Sometimes organisations deliberately invoke disruption as a stimulus to creativity. This is a charitable way of thinking about the restructuring that executives subject their organisations to, although TU's experience is that the harm greatly exceeds the good.

Be ready to take advantage of opportunities.

With options in hand, we can turn adversity into advantage, if we move quickly and confidently into new possibilities. This is "the harder I work the luckier I get", combined with the principle of planning and optimising for the present, both coming to fruition. Our agility gives us speed and innovation. Our resilience and our embrace of failure give us confidence. When the world gives us lemons, we make lemonade.

---

[70] https://ec.europa.eu/jrc/en/publication/managing-complexity-and-chaos-times-crisis-field-guide-decision-makers-inspired-cynefin-framework

How do we survive and thrive in a VUCA world? S&T happens if we:

- Optimise for now.
- Plan for the foreseeable.
- Sense-make all the time.
- Prepare for the adjacent possible.
- Build resilience to the unexpected.
- Build agility to take advantage of it.

"The harder I work, the luckier I get."

Afterword

I'm finishing this book lying on the new improved window seat in our remote mountain hut, our Third Office. Dr Vu is writing million-dollar proposals for major corporations in Vietnam, while snuggled in the warm bed near me (it's a tiny hut).

New Zealand is under COVID restrictions. We haven't been overseas in two years. But business and life have never been better. That personal journey I started this book with is entering a new phase. After years together, we just got married. Cherry is a star in Vietnam. Travel will resume soon. We will uncouple from New Zealand for a while to begin some new adventures. We hope this book inspires you to embrace the "new normal" of the Twenty Twenties, to survive and thrive as we and our clients are. Good luck!

Aroha nui and tạm biệt các bạn.

Rob and Cherry

Rob and Cherry can be found at tealunicorn.com

www.ingramcontent.com/pod-product-compliance
Lightning Source LLC
Chambersburg PA
CBHW052336220526
45472CB00001B/452